THE END OF FOREIGN POLICY?

Britain's Interests, Global Linkages and Natural Limits

Peter Hain

"green alliance...

THE ROYAL INSTITUTE OF
INTERNATIONAL AFFAIRS

Published in Great Britain in 2001

Distributed for the Fabian Society, Green Alliance and the Royal Institute of International Affairs by Plymbridge Distributors Ltd, Plymbridge House, Estover Road, Plymouth, Devon, PL6 7PY. Tel: +44 (0)1752 202301, fax: +44 (0)1752 202333, email: orders@plymbridge.com

ISBN 1 86203 131 2

Cover design by Matthew Link

Printed and bound in Great Britain by Selwood Printing Ltd

The publication of this pamphlet was made possible by generous sponsorship from Rio Tinto plc.

RIO TINTO

CONTENTS

FOREWORD

Most change, in diplomacy as in everything else, comes in small steps. But every so often, we face a seismic shift. The landscape is rearranged beyond recognition. We then need to go back to first principles: to redefine our priorities, and reassess the means by which we pursue them.

As Kofi Annan and others have recognized, we have emerged from the Cold War into just such an episode of dramatic change in world affairs. Globalization is creating new opportunities and new threats. We are beginning to see our national aims against a background of global interests that we all share: the alleviation of poverty and disease; the need to maintain the healthy planetary environment on which, ultimately, we all depend. But to achieve these aims, governments increasingly need to work in new ways, with new partners.

How should Foreign Ministers, and the diplomats accountable to them, react to these new circumstances? This pamphlet brings the new diplomatic agenda into focus, and launches what will be a crucial debate: about the sort of world we are leaving to future generations, and how we can best manage – for Britain and the global community – the problems and opportunities before us.

The Rt Hon. Robin Cook MP
Secretary of State for Foreign and Commonwealth Affairs

PREFACE

Defining trends, especially global trends, is always risky. And *The End of Foreign Policy?* is a brave question to pose, especially for a Foreign Office Minister. But this is a brave pamphlet in many ways, not least because it provides answers as tough as the question it asks.

Its central argument is compelling: that the connections created by globalization in all its forms, and the limits imposed by Nature in all of hers, make the continued pursuit of narrow sovereign or sectoral foreign policy obsolete, or even harmful. National fishing policies have decimated international fisheries. AIDS and drugs policies pursued separately do not work, and so on.

In the context of the new global reality, new approaches are needed that respect natural limits and share the benefits of global linkages equitably. 'Ecologically sustainable development' and 'the globalization of responsibility' are two potential new approaches which Peter Hain advocates. They call on a wide range of actors, from individuals to supranational powers, and from nation-states to business and NGOs, to be prepared to work together in new ways to tackle issues which exceed the capacity of any one of them to deal with on their own. They encourage all parties to recognize policy connections, to anticipate or avoid predictable problems and to align self-interest with shared aims. 'Convergent' policy-making of this kind requires joined-up thinking, regional partnerships among groups of nations, the involvement of all interested players in decision-making, and flexible, transparent international institutions.

But this is not an abstract or Utopian treatise, seeking either perfect global governance or a return to a local idyll. It offers options for action at different socio-political levels and for different constituencies. The UK government can promote global responsibility and sustainable development on the world stage and take relevant action at home, both in the wider economy and within the machinery of government, starting at the Foreign Office. It can help build the capacity for positive change in existing international bodies, such as the World Trade Organization, the UN and the Bretton Woods institutions, and facilitate the transition itself. At a regional level in the South, and among individual disadvantaged nations, the UK and others can help create the ability to participate in the global process, in part by accelerating debt relief and reducing agricultural subsidies in the North.

Media, diplomatic and academic networks could share information on achieving the economic and environmental benefits of resource productivity, and business could help realize them. The sustainable use of water resources will require the cooperation of many groups. The 'Rio Plus Ten' process that culminates in 2002 provides a launchpad for many of these ideas, and many of the stakeholders play a role.

The moment at which a political trend is recognized and a turning point reached is never easy to pinpoint, even with hindsight. But this pamphlet has the potential to capture that moment, not only because of the quality of its ideas, but thanks to the clarity with which they are expressed and presented, and the source from which they spring.

Our organizations are pleased to be part of it, for those reasons, and because the cooperative process by which it was produced exemplifies the very way forward that the pamphlet recommends. Three non-profit organizations, with very different backgrounds, interests and ways of operating – sponsored for this purpose by a major transnational company – have worked together to publish this important and innovative set of arguments, which we believe will contribute substantially to the debate about how best to achieve global responsibility and ecologically sustainable development for all.

Michael Jacobs, *General Secretary, Fabian Society*

Paul Jefferiss, *Director, Green Alliance*

Professor Simon Reich, *Director of Research, Royal Institute of International Affairs*

Andrew Vickerman, *Head of External Affairs, Rio Tinto plc*

ABOUT THE AUTHOR

Peter Hain has been Minister of State at the UK Foreign and Commonwealth Office since July 1999. He was previously a Minister in the Welsh Office and is Labour MP for Neath. Brought up in South Africa until his parents were forced to leave in 1966 because of their anti-apartheid activities, he was a leading anti-apartheid campaigner, as well as a prominent member of the British environmental movement. He is the author of sixteen books.

ACKNOWLEDGEMENTS

My thanks go to a number of people, including officials in the Foreign Office and the Prime Minister's Office, who have kindly contributed ideas and advice to this project. As Foreign Secretary, Robin Cook has given British diplomacy real environmental impetus for the first time. Clare Short and Michael Meacher encouraged me. Although responsibility for the result is mine alone, I am especially grateful to John Ashton, Head of the FCO's Environment Policy Department, and to Tom Burke and Nick Mabey, who have been involved throughout; to Sir John Kerr for his detailed comments on earlier drafts; and to Creon Butler and Harriet Ware-Austin.

The contributions of Rio Tinto plc, the Royal Institute of International Affairs, Green Alliance and the Fabian Society are also much appreciated. Without this unusual partnership, the publication, launch and distribution of this pamphlet would not have been possible.

January 2001   P.H.

'Only connect… live in fragments no longer'
(E. M. Forster, *Howards End*)

1 INTRODUCTION

For a foreign minister to contemplate 'The End of Foreign Policy' may seem like inviting redundancy. It could also risk being confounded – like those whose once fashionable forecasts of 'The End of History' and 'The End of Ideology' proved so premature.

However, we confront new international challenges, driven by growing connections between economies, governments and increasingly active citizens, coupled with rising pressures on the environmental foundations of our societies. In the face of these challenges, the basic goals of foreign policy – to provide stability and security as a foundation for freedom and prosperity – remain the same as ever. But they can no longer be achieved only through the traditional instruments of alliances, treaties, the management of bilateral relations and the creation of intergovernmental organizations. A new dimension is needed.

For example, how can we mobilize against global warming or illegal drug use, when the cause is not the ambition of some hostile power, but the individual consumption decisions of us all? These new threats arise from failures of the system itself. So we need systemic solutions to deal with them.

2 TRANSFORMATION

When I was born – after two thousand centuries of human life – there were two billion people on the planet. Now, just half a century later, there are six billion of us, and the population could rise to eight billion in my lifetime.

We owe this phenomenal growth to our increasing ability to manipulate Nature to meet our needs: for food, health, mobility and comfort. As human knowledge has advanced, a world has unfolded of ever richer possibilities undreamed of even by my parents' generation. But the same forces are also transforming the character of our lives and of our relationships with each other. This is happening at every level from the purely private and local to the fully public and global.

This pamphlet represents a personal attempt to understand the significance for Britain of the changes unfolding around us, from climate change to the Internet, from biotechnology to the mass diplomacy of the anti-landmines campaign and protests against the World Trade Organization at Seattle. It draws on my experience as a Minister of State in the Foreign and Commonwealth Office. And it also draws on a political journey over three decades, from the struggle against apartheid through the early days of British environmentalism to the challenges that global markets pose for employment and industrial regeneration in my South Wales valley constituency of Neath.

What follows is a snapshot of a world in which people and events are becoming linked in ever more complex ways; in which the limits of Nature's ability to respond to our demands increasingly constrains the available policy choices; and in which policies and institutions will, more and more, only function with the active consent of those whose lives they affect. A world defined, in other words, by global linkages, natural limits, and the search for new forms of legitimacy.

Globalization is often portrayed as a single process, rolling like a rising tide over everything in its path. In reality it results from the interplay between separate but intertwined forces. A vast network of satellites, fibre-optic cables and computers carries information and, perhaps even more importantly, images instantaneously to and from the remotest parts of the planet. These technologies have made possible global markets for capital, goods and services, and with them the expanding opportunities of a globalizing world.

Another facet of globalization, however, has been the emergence of agreed global rules for managing our dealings with each other. These rules govern a wide variety of activities, from how we use outer space or the resources of the oceans to common standards for labour or human rights. Two of the most highly elaborated sets of rules are those governing trade, now consolidated inside the World Trade Organization, and those governing the environment, which now run to over 200 separate treaties, including those on the climate and biodiversity.

If the global technologies and markets make possible opportunities, the rules systems define responsibilities. Many of those who are most concerned about the effects of globalization, whether on the planet's cultural diversity or ecological viability, fear that these rules are too weak, are not properly enforced or favour the creation of opportunities over the acceptance of the accompanying responsibilities. These fears are real. But they must not become an excuse for denying to others the benefits that those fortunate enough to live in the rich world are now enjoying.

Today, the imperatives of globalization and the environment present new challenges for foreign policy: challenges that the traditional tools of diplomacy cannot by themselves address. Our overriding aim should be to make available to everyone all the possibilities created by globalization; and to ensure that we pursue those possibilities in ecologically sustainable ways, through policies and institutions that reinforce rather than interfere with each other. We need to develop a shared sense of global responsibility within which to enjoy the new global opportunities, while simultaneously respecting the ever more pressing natural limits that now shape the world. This is now the central challenge of global politics.

British foreign policy has long been noted for its 'suck it and see' pragmatism, and for its corresponding distrust of grand designs. That is a healthy impulse which rightly still conditions our approach to the European project, for example. But it is no longer sufficient if we want to steer a wise course through ever more turbulent global currents ahead.

3   THE DIPLOMACY OF GLOBAL INTERESTS

Traditional diplomacy has been likened to a game of multidimensional chess with many players. Each has separately defined interests, framed largely from within. Sometimes these interests coincide, prompting alliances, often underpinned by military might. But there is little shared vision among all the players, and constant jostling: not everyone can be a winner, nor indeed a loser. Power is divisible and contested. Statesmen from Richelieu to Kissinger have sought to manipulate its balance.

This is the history of modern diplomacy up to the late nineteenth century. The brutal succession of diplomatic failures that then followed taught the world the importance of defusing the causes of conflict as well as managing conflicts themselves. The practices of traditional diplomacy were duly expanded to cover new areas of public policy, as groups of countries began to pool a degree of national power in return for shared benefits.

After two World Wars, a new architecture eventually began to take shape. Its building blocks included the United Nations and its daughter bodies (such as the World Health Organization and the Food and Agriculture Organization), the Bretton Woods institutions (the World Bank, the International Monetary Fund, and the General Agreement on Tariffs and Trade), and regional bodies such as the Common Market in Europe. But even in these more advanced structures, it takes time before national behaviour within the group ceases to reflect purely national definitions of interest. And as a new century begins, the limits of this system are in turn becoming apparent.

How relevant are yesterday's models today, when a computer virus sent out by two students in the Philippines can disable ten million computers worldwide? Or when the costs to us all of not dealing with climate change far outweigh the costs to each of us of cooperating against it?

A defining characteristic of our times is the growing domain of interests that we all share – interests that affect every human being regardless of nationality. These include the stability of the climate; the elimination of poverty and social exclusion, in rich and poor countries alike; the capacity of the trade system to deliver benefits to all; and the defeat of global scourges such as HIV/AIDS, drug abuse and the ever-lurking menace of terrorism.

These goals cannot sensibly be pursued without new forms of engagement and negotiation, in which governments allow more space for others with legitimate contributions to make. Nor can they be pursued separately from each other. The fight against corruption matters as much for the environment as for economic prosperity. Transparent flows of information are as important for human rights as for the efficient allocation of resources. And so on.

I believe that common interests such as these will come to dominate world affairs. Within them, we shall still pursue distinct national aims. But the responsibility of the current generation of world leaders is no longer merely to balance those aims. Instead they must first align the way their nations see their own interests with the new global imperative. Before asking 'How can we use our diplomatic tools to secure maximum national benefit?' they should ask 'How can our nation best contribute to the attainment of the global goals we all share?'

This is not a lapse into naïve altruism, but a hard-headed calculation. Amidst all the new challenges, the central purpose of foreign policy remains reliably constant. Whatever the language used at the time – and foreign policy is peculiarly prone to very arcane language – governments have always been judged by their ability to create secure and stable surroundings for those they govern. Usually, this was understood to include freedom from external aggression, access to reliable supplies of vital materials, and healthy (if no longer captive) foreign markets for domestic products.

The emergence of shared global interests does not alter these goals. But it certainly affects the means by which they can be achieved. For islands at risk of being swallowed by the sea, climate change is as much a threat to sovereignty as a human invasion. But it cannot be prevented by military force. Refugees fleeing political, economic or, ever more often, ecological dislocation press increasingly against whatever barriers nations choose to put around their borders. How effective can a domestic campaign against HIV/AIDs be when, in Britain's case, three-quarters of victims in 1999 were infected while travelling in Africa? In tomorrow's world, stability and prosperity at home will depend above all on the ability of the international community to act together in pursuit of interests that transcend national frontiers.

This point is illustrated by comparison with the last great global interest: stopping the Cold War from becoming a hot war. This was the single most important foreign policy objective for most nations. As seen from Europe the issues were very clear. The Russians had their tanks on our lawn and nuclear missiles all around us, and were imposing authoritarian rule on both their own people and those of their satellites.

The West's response was to build and maintain a network of formal alliances with like-minded governments to contain those beyond the Iron Curtain. At the same time, governments this side of the Curtain had an additional incentive to ensure that the free world was also a prosperous world.

They did this by putting in place a macroeconomic framework designed to facilitate trade and investment, and thereby to raise the Gross Domestic Products of those willing to sign up to the rules of the framework. The promise of prosperity was similarly held out, through the availability of aid from the North, to the poorer South. The coffers were unlocked not entirely from a desire to share prosperity, but also as an inducement to resist the blandishments of the competing ideology. The leading institutional agents of this strategy were the IMF, the World Bank, and the GATT (now the WTO).

For fifty years, this unprecedented combination of military and economic cooperation did roughly what it was designed to do, at least as seen from Western Europe and North America. True, immediate considerations of national security often disrupted and sometimes defeated wider economic aims, especially for those on the periphery. But it was largely as a result of this system that the Cold War ended in a wholly welcome whimper. The economics worked, because in well-managed economies the framework delivered real and widespread prosperity, and because under conditions of less ecological stress, wealth as measured by GDP approximated more closely than it does now to quality of life.

But as we enter the twenty-first century, the challenges are different. We cannot build alliances, at least not of the traditional kind, against global warming, AIDS, terrorism, or the silent conspiracy between those who abuse drugs within our frontiers and those who run the supply chains from outside them. Nor is the existing economic framework any longer sufficient by itself. We need new tools to attack the growing global problem of conspicuous wealth creation at the expense of public welfare, both between rich and poor nations and within them. The only sustainable basis for future wealth creation is one achieved without unacceptable costs in pollution, the irreversible loss of natural capital, the entrenchment of current levels of massive inequality, or the abuse of human rights.

4 FIND THE VILLAIN

Policy-makers – domestic and international – and the institutions they inhabit are equipped to deal with specific problems, relating to policies, places or sectors that can be circumscribed and isolated from other aspects of government. But the new class of global issues is different. Their origins straddle both national and sectoral boundaries in seemingly haphazard ways. Breakdown comes not from a single point of failure, but from weaknesses in the entire system. The problems are joined up, so government must be joined up. No ministry in any government – health, agriculture, fisheries, transport, energy, finance, foreign affairs, defence, industry – can afford not to be thinking about the way climate change might affect its ability to carry out its responsibilities. Likewise, there is no single government department or intergovernmental organization for dealing with climate change, drug abuse and trafficking, AIDS, or intensifying competition for water and fish. Nor could there sensibly be.

System failures of this kind are not easy to recognize. They most often manifest themselves as more familiar problems: a harvest failure here, a flood there, a civil war in one place, food riots in another. In the face of such emergencies, the temptation is to respond only to those difficulties rather than to their underlying causes.

That may, like an aspirin, alleviate the pain for a while; but it will never cure the disease. UN intervention will not by itself stabilize Sierra Leone. As long as the rebels can raise money by selling diamonds from the mines they control, they will continue to pose a threat. Simply sending in troops, as in the past, to keep the peace will not be enough. That is why the British government has been pushing so hard for the international trade in diamonds to be regulated, so as to block that part which finances violence – but without adding to the barriers to international trade which we are working busily to demolish elsewhere.

Colombia is another potentially prosperous and stable country that shows how the cross-connected nature of modern problems limits the impact of traditional foreign policy. Here, the problem arises from the predilections of the coca plant for the local soil and climate, and of Europeans and North Americans for the product. The consequences have been appalling. Governance has been inexorably undermined by the corruption and organized crime that goes hand in hand with the drug trade. Thriving on this institutional collapse, bands of terrorists and insurgents set ever higher standards of barbarism and prevent the political renewal necessary to rebuild the economy and wrest it from the traffickers. For many Colombians, the result has been a life of poverty and terror.

The international community, led by the US, has responded to the symptoms as well as it knows how. It has deployed all the traditional tools of firefighting diplomacy. It has made available copious quantities of financial, political and, in the case of the US, military support. But the hydra seems to grow two new heads every time one is chopped off.

The fumigant that kills the coca plant pollutes the soils and rivers. The coca growers slash and burn further into the forest and, in refining their crop, further pollute the land. This, and the higher rewards for growing coca underwritten by distant consumers, makes it even harder to build new livelihoods based on legitimate crops. More of the rural poor are displaced from their land, making them dependent on the guerrillas, further feeding the spiral of violence and poverty in which the drug lords flourish.

The reality is that the political alliance between the US and Colombian governments has not been remotely as potent as the unspoken one between the drug traffickers and the millions of mostly affluent Americans and Europeans whose taste for cocaine pays the bills. As with so many problems on the new global agenda, the villain turns out in the end not to be a corrupt government, careless corporation, faceless bureaucrat, or greedy gangster – but the millions of daily choices made by individuals with either too little knowledge of, or too little concern for, the consequences.

5   THE DISPERSAL OF POWER

There is another dynamic that compounds these problems. Until fairly recently, the power to shape world affairs lay largely in the hands of national governments, and a small number of those at that. But the emergence of new interest-based coalitions, enabled by modern mobile communications, is fragmenting international power and distributing it in more complex ways.

Governments have themselves been choosing for some time to accept new supranational constraints on their freedom of action, and to pool their sovereignty *upwards*. The two hundred or so international agreements on the environment, the legally binding and justiciable trade rules, and the single European market, all represent voluntary restrictions on national sovereignty in recognition of a wider interest. At the same time, many countries, including Britain, have experienced growing pressure to devolve power *downwards* to increasingly assertive nations, regions and cities.

But power is also moving *outwards* into new configurations that have little to do with governments at any level, or with the physical boundaries that define where they hold sway. A growing number of multinational corporations have incomes that more than match those of most states. The turnover of Wal-Mart is roughly identical to the GDP of Norway. In 1999, the revenue of

General Motors – with 340,000 employees worldwide – exceeded the combined GNP of 45 African countries, encompassing 590 million people (the entire continent except for South Africa, Egypt, Nigeria, Algeria and Morocco).

Meanwhile new forms of political organization are creating new agents of change that can be just as influential as governments or companies. Common-interest communities can coalesce almost overnight over the Internet, and deploy enormous influence on a bewildering array of issues, from Third World debt or landmines to the disposal of oil platforms at sea and GM crops.

Indeed one of the most striking political phenomena of recent years has been the rapid growth of non-governmental organizations and their expanding influence on the world stage. Many of the most prominent of these bodies have origins in Britain – Oxfam, Save the Children, Amnesty International, the World Wildlife Fund (now the Worldwide Fund for Nature). Often more trusted by the public than governments or official bodies, these organizations have given direct expression to the concerns of millions of their supporters through imaginative initiatives which capture media attention and through powerful advocacy. More radical groups such as Greenpeace pursue direct action too. In Britain, almost five times as many people belong to environmental groups as to all the political parties put together.

Some have claimed that these trends signal the decline of the nation-state. But the nation-state has already outlived many of its obituarists. No other entity can pass laws, sign treaties, raise taxes. No other entity can enjoy the legitimacy of a democratically elected government or the right legally to deploy military force.

On the other hand, capital has gone global, taking at least some 'sovereignty' with it, and any notion that democratic accountability can be exercised solely through the nation-state is illusory. So national governments certainly have a harder job than hitherto. Not only must they understand a new and more complex set of problems. To deliver solutions they also have to learn how to form new partnerships with the other, more recent arrivals on the stage. Governments alone cannot conjure up the innovation we shall need to meet our energy and transport needs in climate-friendly ways. Nor can they successfully regulate the modification of genes, nor the system of world trade, without the consent of an ever more disparate range of people and institutions. Nor, on their own, can they establish the 'new ethic of conservation and stewardship' which the United Nations Secretary General Kofi Annan has called for.

Moreover, as governments face diminishing control over events, those they govern want more control over their lives. More affluent, more confident, better educated and better informed, people want more say in the decisions that affect them. And they want to have this say more directly. This will be a less deferential century in every way. The decline we are witnessing in the authority of public institutions in many parts of the world is what happens when people acquire and begin to use the right to choose. A connected world dramatically widens that realm of choice. The institutions will fail if they cannot respond to the changing expectations of the people they serve, or engage the widening constituencies with an interest in their decisions. This is as true of global institutions as it is of national ones.

It is sometimes argued that, as long as the governments that negotiate with each other are themselves democratic, then the process in which they are taking part must, by definition, be so too. But the decisions and complex trade-offs that come out of, say, the trade negotiations are often little debated domestically. Rulings by closed international panels can appear to many as arrogant and arbitrary impositions, especially if they lead to national measures that restrict the economic opportunities of Scottish weavers, French cheese-makers, or others who themselves have no connection with the dispute in question. They may have the form of democratically accountable decisions but that is not how it feels to those they affect. This should not be a surprising consequence of a process in which the force of law is not yet fully balanced by the safeguards of justice.

In today's more demanding circumstances public institutions must go beyond the formal observance of democratic forms and promote public participation and accountability if they are to rebuild and retain public trust. Increasingly, business – often led by British companies – has been showing the way, moving beyond formal legal compliance with environmental and other regulations to engage directly with those affected by their operations.

Those institutions that do not renew and reinforce their legitimacy will eventually stop functioning. This was a lesson the World Trade Organization was given very dramatically in Seattle. As President Clinton recognized at the time, the noisy protestors on the streets were giving expression to anxieties that were much more widely shared. Organized on a global scale via the Internet, the protestors came together to pursue many different and some mutually contradictory causes. But one aim united them all – their concerns should not be left out when trade experts were meeting to decide issues that would affect the choices they wished to make. Governments must not, of course, abdicate negotiating responsibility to any lobby – certainly not to one acting violently – that decides to take to the street. But they should certainly listen when the street is the only platform available from which to raise legitimate questions about what is going on in the negotiating chamber.

Yet, despite the complexity of the new international landscape, its underlying pattern is deceptively simple. The events with which we have to deal are shaped increasingly by the interplay of just two forces: the widening of possibilities that arises from the new linkages between people, and the narrowing of possibilities resulting from the perennial but now starkly apparent limits imposed on us by Nature. It is these two forces that are placing new responsibilities on all of us.

6 LIVING WITH LINKAGES

The floods that devastated Mozambique in early 2000 struck one of the poorest countries in the world and stopped in its tracks an economy that, after years of bitter internal warfare, was just beginning to take off. A succession of disasters in the past two years – in Nicaragua and Honduras, Venezuela, Turkey, India, Madagascar – has overwhelmed the capacity of most of the affected countries to cope and overstretched the capacity of the world to respond. This past year we in Britain were almost paralysed by unprecedented floods many believe to have been the product of climate change. These came on top of popular protests against fuel costs caused by the trebling of world oil prices which also almost brought the country to a standstill. And while Northern Europe has had unprecedented floods, Kenya has had unprecedented drought. Even the mighty United States had to appeal for international help in the face of the wildfire onslaughts in summer 2000.

Such events seem to many of us to be occurring more frequently. Mounting insurance claims suggest that their effects are becoming more devastating. Certainly, we are more immediately aware than ever of what is happening to our fellow human beings, and their lives feel more bound up with our own. We are linked to each other by images and information flashed to our televisions and computers via a constellation of satellites, nearly all of which have taken their place in the sky in the last thirty years. If we want to know more than the nightly news tells us about what is happening elsewhere we can search the Internet at the touch of a button or use our mobile phone to call a friend on the spot almost from wherever we happen to be at the time. I can read the *New York Times* on the Web in London before Manhattan wakes up. A friend in Chennai reads the *Guardian* on his PC at work five hours before it pops through my door at dawn.

Everyone who can tap into these new flows of knowledge and ideas – the established and emerging middle class around the world – lives, in effect, in a shared information space that respects no boundaries. Perhaps these are the beginnings of a global culture. All governments are at least uneasy about this, if only because of the consequences for privacy, crime and public morals. Some see it as a more serious threat. Witness the desperate, but ultimately futile, attempts by China's authorities to dictate what its citizens can and cannot pick up from the Internet, or the turmoil caused in traditional cultures by uncontrollable access to alternative visions of life.

The interconnected world abounds in opportunities. More people are more comfortable than ever before, living secure, healthy, fulfilling lives. But equally, millions more people than ever before live lives of the most abject misery, insecure, ill and unemployed – or starving and dying.

In part, this paradox arises from the sheer numbers of people now on the planet: we have added faster to the poor than to the rich. But it also betrays our inability, and often unwillingness, to share the wealth that flows in such abundance from the opportunities our connected world creates. And not everyone is, or can quickly be, as connected as everyone else. The deepening digital divide is already an important issue on the global agenda. Globalization, like any change, creates losers as well as winners. So our more connected world is certainly not a fairer world.

Not all the new linkages are virtual. Many are all too real. The electronic networks that carry the information that drives investment flows also convey the messages and money that fuel international terrorism and drug trafficking. Pathogens and invasive species hitch rides on the transport infrastructure that carries goods and services to every corner of the world. Brazilians buy cars made in Europe from aluminium smelted in Australia. Those smelters emit carbon dioxide that contributes to climate change throughout the world.

The AIDS crisis in Africa illustrates even more clearly how effectively our new networks can amplify once local problems. More than half of all the sufferers from AIDS live in sub-Saharan Africa and 5,000 die each day. By the end of this decade there may be more than 40 million AIDS orphans in this region. This vicious disease spreads along the transport routes and through the most active people in the economy, destroying disproportionately those who are most needed. A teacher a day currently dies of AIDS in Côte d'Ivoire, a student a week in one of

South Africa's top universities. A fifth of Malawi's MPs in the 1994–99 Parliament died of AIDS. In Zimbabwe, where a quarter of the population are HIV-positive, close to half of an already inadequate health budget goes on AIDS-related treatment.

So a spiral of despair develops. Poverty leads to inadequate health education, which makes the prevention of AIDS more difficult, which removes the skilled and educated from the population during their prime years, which leads to deeper poverty, which fuels instability and insecurity that spills over into neighbouring states, undermining their capacity to deal with AIDS.

In a past, less connected era, a deadly new disease like AIDS might not have become a global scourge. There could be no better example of how, in an interconnected world, local events can have dramatic and unforeseen global consequences. Here, for me, lies the essence of globalization: the way it is creating shared communities of interest and experience that transcend the traditional frontiers of states and the traditional mechanisms of representative government.

7 LIVING WITH NATURAL LIMITS

The linkages that help us to communicate are of our own making. But another potent set of connections binds together from the outside the fortunes of everyone on this planet. These arise from the limits to the capacity of natural systems – the atmosphere, the oceans, agricultural soils, the cycles of freshwater and nutrients – to meet the demands we place on them. It is only in recent years that we have begun to understand that these limits exist, and that we are fast approaching them – indeed in some cases have probably already surpassed them.

Our ability to manage our transactions with the planet around us is usually discussed in the context of environmental or, more rarely, economic policy. Yet I believe these issues go right to the heart of the new diplomacy. Foreign policy will increasingly be about the tensions and difficult choices that arise from environmental stress and competition for resources. In responding, we must not let yesterday's notions of sovereignty and national interest get in the way of solutions that are bound to transcend the limits of those ideas.

For example, the relentless pursuit of cod on the Grand Banks of Newfoundland by heavily subsidized fishing fleets led to a collapse of the fishery in the early 1990s. This provoked a stand-off on the high seas between Spanish and Canadian warships, and an exchange of shots between NATO allies. Fisheries are the main source of protein for over a billion people, most of whom live in poverty. Fishing fleets worldwide have substantially more capacity than they need to remove fish from the oceans in sustainable quantities. Despite a growing framework of legal and political commitments, stocks continue to decline. Unless we rapidly develop a wholly new way of managing the ocean resources we hold in common, further confrontations are unavoidable.

Around the world the advance of industry, intensive agriculture and high-consumption lifestyles is increasing the competition for water. One-third of the human race lives today in water-stressed countries. Take Mexico's recent drought. It ensured a failure to meet contractual commitments to supply Texas with water from the Rio Grande and cost the US economy millions of dollars in lost agricultural revenue. The Middle East peace process showed just how acute an issue water has become when the Israelis and Palestinians agreed to put off consideration of water allocation until after they had settled the 'easier' problems of security and settlements! Egypt has announced that it will resort to war if necessary to stop upstream states disrupting the flow of the Nile on which it so depends.

Tension over water is not new, of course. But in an overcrowded and interdependent world, the stakes are certainly higher than ever before – to the point where there is now emerging, for the first time, a need for an approach to water management based on globally accepted principles.

It is fifteen years since Gro Haarlem Brundtland first

urged us to provide for today's needs without jeopardizing the environmental basis for meeting tomorrow's. Nine years have passed since most of the world's leaders met in Rio at the Earth Summit to proclaim the urgency of meeting that challenge. Since then there has grown up an entire industry of negotiations, dialogues and resolutions, all searching for the elusive secret of sustainable development. If the sheer intensity of traditional diplomatic activity were a reliable measure we would be well on track. But, as Kofi Annan reported to the Millennium Assembly of the United Nations:

> We now face an urgent need to secure the freedom of future generations to sustain their lives on this planet – and we are failing to do it. We have been plundering our children's heritage to pay for unsustainable practices ... our responses are too few, too little and too late.

And, as the evidence accumulates, it is clear that for all the diplomatic effort our environmental defeats are outpacing our victories. We are pushing ever harder on the limits of the planet's capacity to deliver rising real incomes and a better quality of life to our ever-growing population. Without those rising real incomes, equitably spread, we shall not be able to contain the destabilizing effects of a new phenomenon: ecologically entrenched poverty.

8 THE GLOBALIZATION OF RESPONSIBILITY

If those engaged in foreign policy face this new class of international problems – arising from both linkages and limits – what about the solutions?

There is both a *political* challenge and a *policy* challenge. As a matter of politics, we need to articulate and build support for a new set of organizing principles for international (and thus also domestic) affairs: principles that will allow us once again to shape events rather than be buffeted by them. This section offers two such principles. But we also need an entirely new approach to the way we devise policies and build institutions in the light of these principles. That is addressed in the next section.

All human action is governed by a few basic impulses. At the international level, these tend to coalesce into more or less durable drivers of policy: the desire to amass wealth or power, to propagate ideologies or religions, and to achieve macroeconomic growth and free trade. Some of these aims have been overtaken by today's conditions and values; others remain relevant but are insufficient by themselves to meet our new needs. What new principles can we apply in order to make the world of global linkages and natural limits a safe and prosperous place for today's six billion people and their even more numerous descendants?

The concept of sustainable development already provides half of the new vision we need. We have hardly begun to learn how to meet the basic needs of humanity – let alone provide wider access to the quality of life that we in the rich world take for granted – without undermining the ecological basis for tomorrow's well-being. We live at present by borrowing from the future – in effect from our children and theirs – often ignorant that we are doing so and never with any idea of how to repay the debt.

There lies the first political challenge. The aim of ecological sustainability must lie at the heart of all our policies and institutions, both domestic and international. Political leaders must be judged according to their commitment to it.

The other half of the vision, deriving from the new human linkages, has been less clearly articulated but is an equally important component of any new politics of global community: what I call the 'globalization of responsibility'.

Go back for a moment to the social and political consequences of the new links between previously unconnected people. Except in sheer global scale, these consequences are actually not all that different from those of previous expansions in connectivity unleashed by previous advances in technology.

There was a pattern to those changes. New connections created new opportunities for those able to take advantage of them. Others did not do so well. Some found themselves exploited by the beneficiaries. Just as there are today, there were losers as well as winners.

This in turn created new tensions. And out of those tensions arose new policies and institutions, even entire new political movements. Britain's Labour government descended from the effort to give a political voice to those whom the Industrial Revolution had disenfranchised. The laws that protect children in Britain and many other countries from exploitation, and consumers from the abuse of monopolies, have similar origins. So do countless other parts of the legal and institutional foundations for the tolerant, humane and decent society we aspire to.

In essence, new connections create new communities of interdependence. But those that endure then grow into communities in the true sense, by developing shared values and a sense of shared destiny. This growing solidarity becomes embedded in the way the community regulates itself through laws, institutions and political processes. The expansion of opportunity for some is followed by the expansion of responsibility to all.

Something analogous is beginning to happen now. Multinational companies – whose shareholders are among the prime beneficiaries of globalization – are beginning to ask themselves whether they have wider responsibilities to society, for example for the environmental and social consequences of their actions. The answer they are hearing more and more from society is: yes, they do.

But this process has barely begun. And governments, though contributing to it in some areas, are not yet focused on the central message it conveys: that they too have a responsibility to ensure that no nation, community or individual is left permanently excluded from the benefits of globalization, and that effective systems are in place to protect everyone from its risks.

As Clare Short, Secretary of State for International Development, has rightly insisted, globalization is happening: we could not stop it even if we wanted to, any more than we can un-invent nuclear weapons. But, as argued in her recent White Paper, *Eliminating World Poverty: Making Globalisation Work for the Poor*, we can certainly shape it – and we must, if we are to spread its benefits and reduce its risks. To do so, we need to activate all sectors of society, nationally and globally, much as we are beginning to attempt in the cause of sustainable development. But only governments can catalyse the concerted, networked effort this will require. Governments will be judged, in the new interconnected world, by their ability to articulate and respond to this challenge.

Sustainable development and the globalization of responsibility go hand in hand. Neither will be achievable without the other. The pursuit of each enhances the other, since the effort to reach equilibrium with Nature tells us a great deal about how to live with each other in a crowded world, and vice versa. Both demand the same approach to policy-making and, indeed, they impose many common requirements. The entrenchment of human rights is good for the environment, for example because it protects those who expose to public scrutiny people who plunder the environment for their own purposes. Effective bodies to protect forests help the fight against corruption in those countries where corruption and logging go hand in hand. The same corruption keeps the rewards of globalization in the hands of the privileged few.

These examples remind us that the advancement of human rights has much to tell us about how to approach the new agenda. The principle of universality, under which basic rights are inviolable in international law in any jurisdiction, shows that we are capable of seeing our interests in ways that transcend traditional national perspectives. The International Covenant on Economic, Social and Cultural Rights states: 'in no case may a people be deprived of its own means of subsistence'. Later, the Covenant identifies certain fundamental rights centring on 'the right of everyone to an adequate standard of living' and including health, 'adequate food, clothing and housing and the continuous improvement of living conditions'.

So our common struggle for human rights can help us pursue our common interest in a healthy environment. Our safety and prosperity depend on our success on both fronts. This is one reason why we should redouble our efforts to ensure that the principles and laws on human rights to which the international community has subscribed are fully upheld in practice. Beyond that, there are newer questions about whether the legal entitlements relating to how we treat each other can usefully be built upon to deal also with how we treat our environment.

9   BEYOND DIPLOMACY: TOWARDS CONVERGENT POLICY-MAKING

Our current approach to policy-making is divergent, not convergent. Governments set themselves aims, embedded to a greater or lesser extent in a unifying political vision. They then pursue them through streams of policy flowing outwards from their aims, each in a specific area. This is reflected in the very structure of almost all governments, divided as they are into subject-specific ministries. In most cases, and certainly in Britain, communication within ministries – often less than perfect – is far better than between them. Where one policy undermines another, corrections are difficult. They are usually achieved through 'end of pipe' adjustments to minimize the damage rather than through truly integrated approaches capable of securing more than one end at once.

It is for these reasons that Labour has pioneered 'joined-up government': new, cross-cutting forms of policy-making that bring different sectoral interests together before policy is decided, so that all interested parties can work within the same big picture and all have ownership of the resulting decisions. Issues such as poverty, social exclusion and climate change simply cannot be contained within any set of convenient departmental frontiers.

Internationally, much the same applies. National policies on the world stage are driven primarily by the same sectoral departments and the sectoral interests they represent. Nations define their aims largely through national processes, with little reference to the shared global aims that I have identified, and often too little consideration of consistency with other national policies. Convergent diplomacy begins at home, and many of the deepest problems with the current international system have their roots in national processes.

As anyone who has sat through a negotiation at the UN can attest, this encourages a zero-sum approach in which everyone tries to maximize their short-term gains at the expense of others. There is little incentive instead to focus on shared long-term interests in which we shall all lose unless we are willing to look beyond the demands of today's powerful lobbies at home.

As we have seen, climate change, drugs, AIDS and so on are such intractable problems because the traditional policy-making machinery is not capable of tackling problems that have no localized source, but that arise instead from interlinked and highly distributed patterns of human behaviour worldwide. There is no single heart into which to drive the stake.

Convergent policy-making addresses this. It sets out to deal specifically with this emerging category of multi-sectoral, transnational problems, on the basis of the following principles.

Convergent policies recognize that real world problems have many causes, and that our responses to them have many consequences.
Instead of relying on the traditional compartmentalized model with its competing streams of policy, the

convergent approach requires that all relevant policies and the institutions responsible for them contribute to the achievement of the appropriate cross-cutting goals, particularly those dictated by the imperatives of sustainability and global responsibility. Policy-makers should not only account for the consistency of their policies with the goal in question, but should actively find ways of aligning this with their existing aims. Thus further reform of the Common Agricultural Policy should be driven not only by Europe's agricultural needs, together with the interests of European consumers and Third World producers. It must also take account of the consequences of our farming practices for European biodiversity.

Convergent policies encourage new partnerships.
Governments can no longer deliver solutions by themselves. Only business can develop the clean energy and transport technologies necessary to get to grips with climate change, and build markets for them. Only science and the non-governmental sector can provide much of the analysis necessary for wise decisions. So governments must learn to bring these and other partners right into the heart of the policy process, so that their expertise can guide new policies from the start, and so that they have stronger incentives to play their part in what is then required.

That is why in the Foreign Office we now have secondees from business, the non-governmental sector, developing countries and other government departments working on the environment and human rights alongside career diplomats.

Convergent policy-making has to be transparent.
If we want others to share our goals, they must be able to see that we mean business and have nothing to hide. If we disagree with them, we must be willing to debate the disagreement in the open, rather than fighting rearguard actions to protect weak policies from scrutiny. There are new examples every day of why this simple principle will increasingly lie at the heart of successful governance.

European publics became hostile to genetically modified crops and foods partly because industry tried to make them commonplace without prior public debate about the consequences for food safety and the environment. I had a role in organizing the international conference on genetically modified food in Edinburgh in early 2000. Its conclusions could help to build a firmer international foundation for regulating this technology. We insisted on giving a voice to all with a legitimate interest, whatever their point of view: from Greenpeace to Monsanto. Some feared that this would result in confusion and even confrontation of the kind we saw at Seattle. Instead, perhaps for the first time in any high-profile international discussion of this emotive issue, all played a constructive part, and all had a hand in the conclusions that emerged.

These attributes – transparency, partnerships, and the alignment of different goals – in turn allow convergent policy-making to operate through solution-focused networks. As we have seen, in an interconnected world, networks are increasingly powerful agents of change. They can bring to bear on a single issue the energy and imagination of diverse individuals and organizations around the world. They embody all the principles so far described. They are the quintessential vehicle for convergent policy-making. They form to tackle specific issues and are not limited to those with particular constitutional roles, but are open to all who can contribute to finding and implementing solutions.

Others, particularly in the non-governmental sector, have seized more quickly than governments the opportunities offered by such networks to define common aims, to share information about them, and to drive change. Governments and the international institutions in which they have a stake now need to catch up. Governments can use their authority and convening power to create new networks and to animate and legitimize existing ones.

Convergent policies recognize that we live in a complex and unpredictable world.
So they take account of downstream consequences. At present we respond to immediate problems with strategies designed primarily to deal with those problems. We are just beginning to learn that we need also to assess the possible side-effects, now and later, of these strategies.

Take a topical example – one of the gravest dangers we now face and one that is incidentally tailor-made for a convergent response: that new strains of antibiotic-resistant bacteria will render us once again as vulnerable as we were in the Middle Ages to death from infection. One of several unwise practices that has contributed to this risk has been the use of antibiotic supplements in animal feed in order to fatten livestock more quickly. The risk that this might promote microbial resistance to antibiotics was identified, at least as a theoretical possibility, before the practice began. But the message was ignored.

Even today, our procedures for identifying and responding to risk make it difficult to take full account of such possibilities. And some aspects of them, including a narrowly and traditionally defined concept of 'sound science' underpinning trade rules, make it even harder. The European Union could not ban imports of antibiotic-fed livestock without opening itself to challenge, and possibly sanctions, under the trade rules.

Another tragic example is the case of accidental poisoning now threatening up to 85 million Bangladeshis, perhaps the greatest environmental catastrophe ever to hit a modern nation. Back in the 1970s, lack of access to clean water was a major cause of death and disease. The response – and at the time it seemed like a breakthrough in appropriate technology – was to sink some three million simple tube-wells, to tap the abundant supply of apparently safe groundwater. Unfortunately, nobody tested this water for natural contaminants. It turned out that, in many parts of the country, local groundwater contains high concentrations of arsenic. At first, as this insidious poison builds up in the body, there are no noticeable consequences. Only after ten years or more do the first symptoms appear, by which time the damage may well be irreversible, or in many cases fatal. An entire generation now faces death or chronic illness due to cancers of the skin, bladder and lungs, and damage to other tissues including the nervous system. Meanwhile, the wells are still in place. Alternatives are now urgently being sought. But for most in the affected areas, the only available water remains contaminated.

Convergent policies seek to prevent problems before they arise.
In an interconnected world, the costs of dealing with a crisis once it has erupted can be far higher than those of avoiding it in the first place. This applies particularly where, as in the case of human conflict or climate change, the consequences of the crisis are likely to be irreversible. So we should put a higher premium on prevention, and be willing to go to greater lengths to achieve it.

An example is the need for a regional approach to water management in Central Asia. The five regional states face increasing competition for scarce water. Current trends and policies, if uncorrected, will generate growing tension between them. Instability in this part of the world will not only cause suffering and environmental damage. It will also hinder our efforts to work with the governments concerned to obstruct the transit through the region of drugs destined for sale on British streets. So we have a strong interest in doing all we can to consolidate stability there. Hence our attempt last year through the Organization for Security and Cooperation in Europe to engage the republics together on water, and our support for the EU's continuing efforts to facilitate the necessary regional approach.

Convergent policies have built-in resilience.
Many of the threats we have considered illustrate our rising vulnerability to shocks that are often unforeseen even if usually foreseeable. Disasters often take a heavier toll because people have chosen or been forced by

36

poverty to live in the path of landslips made more likely by hillside deforestation. New computer viruses can destroy billions of dollars of assets at the click of a mouse. Corruption exposed in a small bank on one side of the world can set off financial shock waves that eliminate thousands of jobs on the other.

These new vulnerabilities are the direct consequence of globalization and the new interdependences it creates. If we want to protect ourselves from them, we need to build this aim into all the processes by which we govern ourselves, at all levels and in all sectors, from town planning to the design and tasking of global institutions. An example of a non-resilient policy, as we found out across Europe during the petrol crisis in autumn 2000, is 'just-in-time' delivery.

Finally, convergent policy-making reflects the world as it is.
The traditional format of intergovernmental negotiations – especially in the UN where states negotiate in blocs some of whose origins lie in the Cold War – perpetuates a simplistic, 'primary colour' vision of a world now long obsolete.

In particular, the distinction between 'developed' and 'developing' countries is one of the greatest obstacles to convergence. The very term 'developing' is patronizing, suggesting that the development path taken by more 'advanced' countries is a model that others should adopt. In fact, many highly industrialized, high-consumption countries offer more examples of mistakes to avoid than wise policies to copy. No country planning a new transport system would like to end up inheriting the dilemmas and unforeseen costs that has made transport as politically contentious as it is in Britain today. For our part, we would do well to ask how we can put in place the kind of clean, reliable, customer-friendly public transport that has made such a name for Curitiba in Brazil.

10 CONVERGENCE IN PRACTICE

These general principles are all very well. But how can they be made to work in the real world of tough political choices? It would take another pamphlet (at least) to begin answering that question. But let me at least offer an illustration.

All governments face dilemmas between the immediate pressures of economic management and the longer-term requirements of environmental responsibility. So, increasingly, do many companies. If convergent policy-making is to have practical value, it should help resolve such conflicts.

To do so, we first need to ensure that reliable information is available about the environmental costs of alternative courses of action. Often, these costs are hidden, or thinly spread over a wide and politically silent constituency. By making them explicit, and building them into the calculations of cost and benefit that influence decisions, we can immediately shift the balance in favour of greater environmental responsibility.

But better information by itself is not enough. We also need to remove the barriers to choice, so that environmentally responsible products and services are available without the cost premiums now too prevalent. And governments need to do more to put in place incentive systems that reward environmentally sustainable choices.

After doing all these things, we may still face problems. The quest for sustainability is an exercise of political transformation, and in any transformation there are losers. Effective action against climate change is not going to favour the global coal industry. So we also need adjustment mechanisms that acknowledge the legitimate needs of those – individuals, constituencies, companies – who will inevitably be penalized through no fault of their own, to help them adapt to the new circumstances.

All this will require vision, imagination, and leadership. But policies already exist, and are continually being refined, to deal with all the needs I have described.

The legal right of access to environmental information is enshrined for citizens of Europe in the Aarhus Convention. Systems of green accounting, such as that recently adopted by the Philippines government, bring environmental costs and benefits more clearly into the accounts of nations and companies. Environmental labelling and certification, from timber to fish, broaden the range of choice, and create rewards in the marketplace for environmentally sustainable activity. Market mechanisms, such as tradeable emissions permits or fishing quotas, reduce the costs of environmental compliance, and spread them efficiently across an economy. Meanwhile, the challenge of helping losers adjust to change is of course as old as politics itself.

So a toolkit is available, even if it still needs to be applied more widely. Up to now, such mechanisms have been put to use predominantly within national economies. A challenge for diplomacy will be to develop common international tools that reward environmental responsibility without putting individual nations at a competitive disadvantage. Nowhere is this process further advanced than across the European Union, which receives far less credit than it deserves for the strides it has taken to develop common approaches to environmental problems.

11 LOCAL OR GLOBAL? A FALSE CHOICE

Some claim there is a far simpler solution. All we need to do is return to an imagined (and wholly illusory) golden age of pastoral self-sufficiency. Is not the identity of the villains perfectly clear: globalization itself, and the global market capitalism it has enabled, the multinationals who profit from it and the financiers, public and private, who sign the loans? Away with the lot of them, and we can reconstruct local communities, markets, farming systems and so on that provided so well for humanity in the past.

This characterization may be somewhat unfair, but it embodies a tradition of market-garden Utopianism running from Rousseau and his forebears to Schumacher and Monbiot. Today, Colin Hines is a compelling advocate for this view, urging us to 'protect the local, globally', from behind an intricately constructed set of local, national and regional barriers to trade and investment. Many of the deficiencies he identifies in our current systems for measuring and producing welfare are, as I have argued, perfectly real. His call to defend the diversity of communities and cultures has a powerful attraction at a time when that diversity is increasingly threatened. The problems he poses must be addressed honestly, and not dismissed.

But that does not validate the prescription. To single

out one form of exchange – cross-border trade – and identify with it the ills of an age is to deny the very complexity and richness he claims to support. If information and ideas are to flow freely around the world (as Hines accepts they must), then so will goods, investment and people. The attempt to prevent this – to pick and choose between what is allowed and what is not on the supply side of globalization – is doomed to fail. But the attempt itself would be an unforgivable assault on choice and opportunity, and therefore on freedom.

Burma provides a cautionary example of what can happen when the doors are slammed shut and self-sufficiency is taken to extremes. Democracy cuts both ways. Those who wish to embrace change (whether it comes as a consequence of globalization or anything else) have the same rights as those who would rather resist it. When those rights are denied in a closed society by putting up barriers to 'protect the public', the real purpose of the exercise is more often than not to preserve the power and privileges of an insecure elite.

The lesson is this. We have seen already that blind faith in inevitably imperfect markets is not going to deliver sustainability or the globalization of responsibility. But nor is an equally misguided faith in the selective partitioning of those markets. These extreme options may make attractive slogans to rally the ideological troops. But they are equally irresponsible, as they do nothing to address either the real problems of people on the ground, or the need for a new diplomacy.

The fact is that if we want long, healthy lives for ourselves and our children, we need well-regulated and fair global markets, providing global technologies, global ideas and a shared sense of global destiny. Without them there is no hope of providing African villages with climate-friendly energy, or of freeing ourselves from the scourges of AIDS and malaria, or of feeding the eight billion or more mouths over the coming generation. There is no way back. The real task is to find the right way forward.

This is not to appeal to some equally Utopian, equally unattainable vision of global government. That would be to succumb to another version of the same fallacy: the idea that all we need to do is to identify once and for all the right level at which to organize ourselves – whether by retreating behind the village stockade, or by pinning our hopes on some omniscient global authority.

The message from convergent policy-making is that action at one level will never be enough to deal with the challenges I have described. The goals of sustainability and globalized responsibility are so overriding that they need to become all-pervasive, to imbue what we do at every level, in every sector and in every place. They are synonymous with the drive to deliver better lives that is at the heart of all healthy politics.

12 BRITAIN AND THE NEW DIPLOMACY

How should Britain respond to the new circumstances? We depend as much as any nation on what happens outside our borders: on the stability, security, and prosperity of others, and on the global environmental quality on which those conditions in turn depend. We are as vulnerable as any not only to the disruption of markets overseas, but also to the effects of climate change, drug trafficking, and migration.

We also have powerful tools we can apply in pursuit of sustainable development and the globalization of responsibility. No other nation is better connected to the existing networks of global governance. Britain is a Permanent Member of the UN Security Council, and a member of the EU, NATO, the Commonwealth and the Group of Eight industrialized countries. English has become the international language of IT and business. We have a global presence, through our 223 overseas posts, and through the global reach of British companies, scientists, NGOs and so on. Many of these bodies are themselves at the enlightened forefront of the response to the new challenges.

First we should add Britain's voice to those who are already speaking out about the challenges I have set out here. Foremost among these is Kofi Annan. In his *We The Peoples* Report to the Millennium Assembly, the UN Secretary General spelled out more clearly than anyone had before the tasks now facing the international community. He pointed to the need to make the benefits of globalization accessible to all, and called for 'a new ethic of global stewardship' which puts the environment at the heart of all policy processes. We should join him in encouraging governments, political parties, the media, civil society and other sectors to debate these issues, and to forge a new international consensus based on sustainability and global responsibility.

We should also examine critically what we are doing at home to promote convergent responses, and to take full advantage of the means available to us to contribute to global solutions. The Labour government's recent White Paper on globalization and development is an important step forward in truly joined-up thinking about how to alleviate poverty in the world I have described. The Labour manifesto will take these ideas further and extend them into other areas. But this will be a continuing process: we shall never be able to say we have finished it.

In the Foreign Office, we should as always guard against the temptation to see 'good relations' (whatever that may mean) with country X as an end in its own right rather than as a means to pursue the kind of wider interests I have identified (as well as more traditional ones such as export promotion). We should also ask whether we try hard enough to understand and respond to the new challenges, and whether our structure, with its traditional stress on the UK's dealings with specific countries and institutions, is optimally geared to doing so. As the information links to our posts in the field improve, there will be a case for dismantling the geographically oriented departments that form the backbone of the FCO structure. We shall increasingly be able to devolve their functions to our posts while strengthening our ability at the centre to use those posts in support of cross-cutting objectives in areas such as the environment, conflict prevention and human rights.

A frustration for me as an FCO Minister has been that the FCO machine is geared to responding to new circumstances mostly by incremental shifts in emphasis. Except in the event of conflict or catastrophe – when it is in a class of its own – it is not well equipped to deliver step changes in the distribution of its effort, in response to the priorities that Ministers set. We cannot effectively meet the needs I have described without such a strategic reorientation. But I accept that Ministers are less good at acknowledging the necessary corollary, given finite resources: it is harder to agree to reductions in effort elsewhere than to bang the drum for more on the major new issues.

Next, we should work energetically with the international institutions to which we belong, to strengthen their capacity to define and act upon interests that we all have in common, and to become more sensitive to the indirect consequences of their decisions, outside the specific sector they are designed to address. This impulse is already transforming some of those institutions thanks to the leadership of people such as Kofi Annan,

Jim Wolfensohn at the World Bank and Klaus Töpfer at the UN Environment Programme.

But there is a long way to go. For example, IMF Structural Adjustment Programmes will need to take fuller account of their environmental and social impacts: difficult at present because the IMF recently had only two people working in Washington on the environment. Many international bodies will also need to become more transparent; those that prosper will be the ones that take the initiative to do so. This will be particularly important for those bodies, such as the World Trade Organization, that are involved in the adjudication and settlement of international disputes.

Underlying all this is the larger question of whether the existing panoply of international bodies and processes is as suited to the challenges of the next generation as it has proved to those of the last one. I am not arguing that Britain should necessarily seek to tear down the existing international architecture and rebuild it according to a new blueprint. But we should all try harder to allow institutions to evolve – including, if they have outlived their usefulness, to make way for more effective successors. Above all, we must make sure that the twin goals of sustainability and global responsibility are at the core of all institutional mandates; and that the barriers between international bodies operating in different sectors become much more permeable than they are in many cases today.

The debate about how to align our aims in the environment and trade illustrates this. The case is sometimes made for the creation of a World Environment Organization.

Some of those who make it see it as a way of reducing the pressure on the trade machinery to take account of environmental concerns. But this misses the point. Whatever the arguments for a WEO (and I am sympathetic), we can only bring these two sets of objectives into alignment by adjusting the interaction between them. This means that with or without a WEO, the World Trade Organization will need to understand and respond to environmental concerns – just as the bodies through which we pursue our environmental aims need to take account of their consequences for trade.

Some argue that the WTO should not try to set rules on the environment. But the problem is that it cannot avoid doing so. For instance, WTO judgments relating to issues from trade in shrimps to aircraft noise draw lines in the sand for the environment as much as for trade.

This goes to the heart of convergent policy-making: the connections between bodies that make or implement policy matter as much as the identities of the bodies themselves. And what goes for the WTO applies equally to the Bretton Woods bodies and across the UN family. All need to align their operations with the underlying requirements of sustainable development and global responsibility. This is not an attempt to avoid hard choices, nor to place impossible new demands on bodies not qualified to respond to them. The point is that these are survival requirements. They can only be met if they are embraced by all whose behaviour impacts on them.

The Economist and others have argued that for the WTO or the World Bank to embrace environmental aims amounts to pandering to unelected pressure groups. In fact, issues such as this are confronting these bodies because of the real impacts on real people of what they do. NGOs have played a vital role both in identifying the problems and in offering solutions, even if their voices are sometimes strident and some of the proposals from the wilder fringes would make matters worse. But the argument of *The Economist* would lose even its super-ficial appeal if elected politicians themselves took up Kofi Annan's challenge with greater vigour.

This is one area where Britain can make an enormous contribution. Because of our uniquely pivotal role as a member of the key international bodies from the EU to the UN Security Council, we can put the questions I have raised in this pamphlet on their agendas. We can energize the debate about them through our links not only with other governments but also with civil society, business, the media, and others who have a stake in the conclusions of that debate.

Linked to this is the capacity of other nations to parti-cipate fully in global governance and to relate national policies to international aims. For example, a country that cannot monitor its greenhouse gas emissions can hardly be expected to play a proactive part in the climate negotiations. This kind of capacity gap is another reason for the post-Seattle blockage in the trade negotiations.

Britain can help address it. We can, and should, make this a priority for our diplomacy and, through convergent policies, for our international profile in other areas. Our aid programme is one key tool. And we can encourage our EU and other partners to do the same. In pursuit of sustainable development and global responsibility there is no more urgent task than to build up the collective capacity of the global community to participate in global processes. Without this, those processes themselves will have little significance.

13 SUSTAINABLE SOLUTIONS

One way to approach the challenge of sustainable development is to ask how we can derive economic benefit from maintaining or restoring environmental quality. If we could identify all the opportunities to do that, and disseminate for application elsewhere the results of successful initiatives, we would be making real progress. The New York City authorities recently found, for example, that it would be cheaper and more effective to purify the city water supply by buying and restoring degraded forest in the Catskill Mountains than by building a new water treatment plant. In how many other settings could that particular lesson in harnessing environmental quality be applied?

One response to this might be to establish a virtual network for debate, open to all, to share information about such 'sustainable solutions'. There would be obvious roles in this for the BBC, the British Council, and the Open University. All have experience of using virtual networks to share the benefits of knowledge. Likewise, LEAD International, our partner in environmental secondments from developing countries (just relocated from New York to London), could also contribute through its expanding network of alumni who are putting the lessons of sustainability into practice in all walks of life around the world. So I invite the leaders of these and other interested bodies – whether based in Britain or elsewhere – to join me in considering the possible benefits of such a network, and how it might be established.

Clean energy

Energy brings together the twin challenges of sustainable development and globalized responsibility. Communities without access to clean, reliable energy supplies cannot participate in the new global community. That is why at the UK's suggestion G8 leaders at the Okinawa Summit set up a Task Force to identify and help overcome the barriers to the more rapid dissemination of clean energy technologies, particularly to poor communities remote from national power grids.

But we can do more. I am particularly keen that we should do all we can to help Africa develop and spread the benefits of clean energy technologies. The need to rely on indoor open fires for cooking and heating has made chronic respiratory disease a constant accompaniment to poverty across Africa south of the Sahara. Where it has been introduced, cheap clean electricity empowers those who have it. It provides light at night and access to the digital world. It extends the opportunities of education and of family life, and creates new livelihoods. Outside South Africa, just 9 per cent of Africans have access to electricity; 533 million do not. A major barrier is the prohibitive cost of fixed infrastructure across huge distances to remote areas. Stand-free technology is therefore optimal. The one thing Africa does not lack is sun. So, with the assistance of new global diplomacy and the donor institutions, photovoltaic power could be made more widely available in Africa as a key objective of development assistance.

Solar technology could really take off in African conditions, providing enough electricity for lighting, heating and communications – and even more creatively, refrigeration for vital drugs in remote rural areas. Prepayment systems being pioneered in a joint venture between Eskom and Shell covering 6,000 homes in South Africa's Eastern Cape province could avoid prohibitive capital costs, which in any case will come down with economies of scale if a new African market for solar energy develops.

So again, to complement what we are doing in the G8, I invite business and financial leaders to explore, with our government, and with the governments of the countries concerned, what we can do together to address the energy needs of the rural poor in Africa. Donor nations, the private sector and host governments should form a new alliance. We need new private/public partnerships to help power Africans to prosperity while improving their environment and that of us all.

Regional water partnerships

Water is equally critical for sustainable development, for the relief from poverty which must be the first step towards globalization of responsibility, and for international stability.

The forthcoming 'Rio Plus Ten' Earth Summit will be an opportunity for world leaders to focus on the need to ensure easy access to adequate supplies of clean water, and to respond with innovative solutions to the increasing competition for this precious resource. At the heart of such solutions will be new partnerships bringing together government, business, NGOs and others – perhaps across groups of countries dependent on shared sources of water.

I support those who want to put water high on the agenda of Rio Plus Ten. There is no other issue that brings together so clearly all the challenges we face, and that calls so clearly for convergent responses based on a shared global strategy. I invite all those with an interest to work with us in the British government to develop such a strategy in advance of Rio Plus Ten.

Building regional capacity

Better global cooperation depends on the capacity of countries to participate, judging and articulating their national interests and bringing to bear the insights that are visible from their distinctive perspectives. Without such informed participation many countries, not surprisingly, feel uncomfortable about signing up to new international obligations. This slows down the system of global governance and obstructs the emergence of innovative solutions.

This problem arises in a multitude of areas including trade, the environment, development and health. Currently a plethora of different donors fund attendance at international meetings, as well as many types of 'capacity-building' activity. The initiatives of different donors are not always well coordinated. Much of the resulting activity takes scarce government officials away from their posts. In some countries more environment officials attend international meetings (for which donors pay) than implement national policies (for which they do not.) There is no mechanism for retaining knowledge and experience once the official concerned moves on.

A more sensible approach would be for donors to cooperate in building regional centres for policy development and capacity-building. Countries could second staff to these centres to work on priorities chosen by the regional partners themselves. The centres – perhaps based on existing regional institutions – would cover economic, social, and environmental themes and so provide opportunities for policy integration. Funding would also be available to replace the seconded staff.

Such an approach would strengthen regional cooperation, create sustainable networks for capacity-building, and be far more efficient for donors. The Rio Plus Ten preparations will be a good opportunity to take this idea forward, with the Southern African Development Community perhaps a starting point.

14 CONCLUSIONS

I have tried to sketch out a vision for the new diplomacy. In doing so, I have deliberately paid little attention to the old agenda, though it is still there. I am certainly not trying to argue that we now live in a world beyond hard political choices, negotiation between governments, and the management of conflicting interests. The case I am making is that these now need to be approached in different ways, reflecting interconnectedness and the new global interests that have taken shape alongside more traditional national ones. But even in the case of the latter, hardly a week goes by without a new illustration of the need for convergent approaches. The BSE saga is one recent reminder of the value of transparency, precaution, and listening to everyone with interests at stake.

Some might respond that the adjustments we need to make are, in essence, marginal; that the fundamentals of governance are in reasonable shape, and capable of rising to the new challenges. I do not believe that. The challenges I have described are novel in nature, wholly unprecedented in scale and complexity, and urgent. Never before have we had to face, for example, the possibility that half of all species will be wiped out within the next human lifetime, with appalling consequences for the ecosystems we depend upon. Previous civilizations have of course faced analogous local threats. They failed to deal with them. That is why they are not around now: they did not perceive until too late that they had crossed a one-way threshold.

But leadership is at least in part about anticipating critical moments, and explaining convincingly how and why the future cannot be built on the template of the past. My argument here starts with the recognition that this task is becoming more pressing, and more complex.

And at the heart of this complexity lies the blurring, sometimes to vanishing point, of the familiar distinctions between the interests of different nations, and indeed between domestic and foreign policy. Hence the – only partially provocative – title of this pamphlet. That is a reality of nature and of politics in a world of linkages. Britain's influence in the world, and its ability to secure its domestic interests, will depend on how well we adjust to that new reality.

For example, I believe that an important part of UK *'foreign'* policy in the coming decades – in terms of real impacts on the daily lives of people across the world – will be our *domestic* efforts to reduce emissions of the greenhouse gases causing climatic change.

These issues also raise the broader question of how to harness the power of the market-place to achieve our social goals. The market is a human construct, not a force of nature, and so is subject to human intervention: we can shape it as we wish. It must always be a servant, never a master. Its imperatives must never become an excuse to override basic human rights – or undermine our children's ecological security. The *globalization of opportunity* which our generation is lucky enough to be experiencing must be accompanied by a *globalization of responsibility*.

Part of this must also be a recognition by the rich countries of their economic responsibilities. There is little serious prospect of getting poorer countries to engage in this agenda if they remain crippled by debt and strangled by discriminatory terms of trade. So our Labour government's drive to achieve early 100 per cent debt relief for the poorest countries must be taken forward globally. Similarly the many poor countries heavily dependent on agriculture must have fair access to rich markets. Agricultural subsidies amounting to $300 billion a year in OECD countries alone equal Africa's entire GDP. High tariffs, anti-dumping regulations and technical barriers to trade in industrialized countries cost sub-Saharan African countries $20 billion annually in lost exports – $6 billion more than they receive in aid. This has to be addressed – albeit again with big domestic impacts politically, socially and economically upon rich countries such as Britain.

Previously, responsibility for foreign policy resided in an elite group of specialist diplomats – experts in negotiation and maintenance of long-term bilateral relationships. But tensions arising from declining water tables in the Middle East, collapsing fish stocks in the Atlantic and persistent drought in East Africa will not be solved at the conference table. Only precautionary interventions on the ground to prevent root causes and build resilient systems of governance can provide long-run stability. This task requires the specialized skills of all government departments – and the committed and innovative involvement of non-government actors in business and civil society. And the best diplomats are studying this new agenda, and learning to tap into those skills and wider talent.

Much international diplomacy – whether on arms control, trade or finance – relied in the past on national governments for legitimacy. Agreements between democratic – or at least sovereign – governments were regarded as legitimate by definition. In many cases citizens took little interest. In some, they came to be excluded in a way that would not be defensible in national politics.

This approach is no longer tenable. Many different groups are now asking for direct voices at the diplomatic table. In the campaigns on landmines and debt, non-governmental actors became major drivers for agreement, raising the political temperature and coordinating action across borders. At Seattle and Prague we saw what happens when groups do not believe they are being heard.

It is no longer possible for governments to make difficult decisions internationally, and then deny responsibility for their impact when they return home. Decisions will become increasingly transparent – putting immense pressures on governments to explain their actions to the electorate.

In this new world multilateral and regional relationships will become more vital than bilateral ones.

Perhaps Foreign Ministries will be renamed 'Departments of Global Affairs' – as the concept of 'foreign' becomes ever harder to define. The skills required of diplomatic staff will multiply, as they are increasingly involved in more technical and complex policy-making – and with more diverse and demanding actors.

International policy will no longer be split into arbitrary compartments. Rather, work will centre on 'convergent' policy solutions which provide gains for all actors. Networks will form around these issues where all with an ability to contribute, or a stake in the problem, will work towards solutions. These networks will challenge governments to 'join up' their national policy-making processes, reassess whom they work with and find constructive ways of working with more nimble and dynamic partners.

International organizations will have to become more permeable to participate effectively in these new networks. They will have to build stronger and more explicit partnerships with other bodies, and reject the counter-productive turf wars of the past.

The formal international architecture will have to become stronger, but also more equitable, transparent and innovative. Rich countries will have to invest in the capacity of weaker and smaller countries to participate, even if this seems to go against their short-term interests. Otherwise the whole international system will grind to a halt through an obstructionism born of incapacity.

In the process we will see an end to traditional foreign policy and the evolution of a new foreign policy based upon global linkages, recognizing natural limits, and embracing global responsibility; a foreign policy for a world in which there is no longer any such place as abroad.